WINNING

The Financial Planning Game

*Understanding the Essentials
of Personal Finance*

Ethan Schmidt, CFP®, CRPC®

Las Vegas, Nevada

Published by King & Justus Books
2620 Regatta Drive, Suite 102
Las Vegas, NV 89128
www.kingandjustusbooks.com

Visit the author's website at
www.catalystwealthmgmt.com

First Edition
ISBN: 978-1-7349386-6-1 (eBook)
ISBN: 978-1-7349386-7-8 (Softback)

Managing Editor: Tiffany Zachary
Cover Design by Aaron Schmidt

TABLE OF CONTENTS

Chapter One: Financial Planning:
A Strategic Game.. 2

Chapter Two: Budgeting:
The Annoying Necessity 4

Chapter Three: Credit Scores, Debt,
And Interest Rates: The Three
Misunderstood Amigos................................ 6

Chapter Four: Building Wealth:
Construction Ahead.....................................13

Chapter Five: Investments:
The All-You-Can-Eat-Buffet.........................23

Chapter Six: Estate Planning:
Preparing For The Inevitable...................... 28

Chapter Seven: Life Insurance:
The Greatest Gift 39

Chapter Eight: Disability Insurance:
Protecting The Most Valuable Asset...You ...50

Conclusion...53

About The Author.......................................54

CHAPTER ONE

Financial Planning: A Strategic Game

"WINNING the Financial Planning Game" is an eye-opening and distinctive reading experience. I cut through the fat and get straight to the juicy "need to know" information. Most people cringe, snore, or sweat when the phrase "Financial Planning" is uttered. Usually, reviewing one's finances takes a backseat and is often neglected. However, this necessary responsibility can be perceived as an exciting strategy game.

Games like chess and monopoly have characteristics comparable to planning. These include fact-finding, problem-solving, and execution. Before playing, competitors ask themselves, "How do I position myself to win?" The successful players think multiple steps ahead, leverage their resources, and take calculated risks. Let's dust off the financial planning board game, roll the dice, and start playing.

CHAPTER TWO

Budgeting: The Annoying Necessity

Budgeting irritates everyone! Feeling confident as the cashier swipes your credit card, buying another round of drinks, or paying for concert tickets is empowering. Acknowledging the significance of saving money develops the mentality to attain financial success. Money doesn't define who you are, but it provides personal security, creates opportunities, and offers philanthropic possibilities.

Being disciplined, consistent, and committed are necessary qualities that sustain good budgeting habits. Implementing this four-step process leads to positive cash flow and prepares you for unexpected twists and turns:

1. Determine monthly and annual fixed expenses

2. Eliminate unnecessary expenses

3. Create an emergency fund (3-6 months of expenses)

4. Pay off high-interest-rate debt when possible

CHAPTER THREE

Credit Scores, Debt, and Interest Rates: The Three Misunderstood Amigos

Strategically managing and leveraging debt can be advantageous. Benefits include obtaining assets, tax deductions, and payment flexibility. To borrow funds at a favorable interest rate, you need a good credit score. This score represents your financial track record. Whether it's purchasing a home, car, or insurance, the financial institution evaluates the risk of accepting you as a client.

Figure 1 represents the elements of a credit score:

Figure 1

Credit Score

Payment History 35%

Creditors assess on-time, late, and missed payments.

Amounts Owed 30%

By using the majority of the credit limit that is allotted to you, lenders might assume you're overextended, which could indicate a higher risk of default.

Length of Credit History 15%

The longer duration of responsible credit use, the better the score.

Credit Mix 10%

Your score can increase with different combinations of credit (mortgage, car loan, credit card).

New Credit 10%

Opening several new accounts at once may cause your score to drop, signifying a possible financial dilemma.

Based upon having a **good to an exceptional** credit score, high borrowing limits, low-interest rates, and a greater approval potential become available.

Credit Score Ranges:

Exceptional	800-850
Very Good	740-799
Good	670-739
Fair	580-669
Poor	300-579

Debt and interest rates are like peanut butter and jelly: you can't have one without the other. Designing a debt and interest rate reduction strategy is another crucial piece of the financial planning game.

Below are two common scenarios:

Scenario 1:

Credit card interest rate	15%
Mortgage interest rate	4%
Student loan interest rate	2.5%

Problem: High-interest rate credit card

Solution: Pay off the credit card as soon as possible to reduce interest and improve cash flow. Also, try to refrain from withdrawing retirement money due to penalties and taxes.

Scenario 1a:

Problem: High-interest rate credit card with no available cash

Solution 1: Borrow money against low-interest equity sources and use it to eliminate the credit card debt. A home equity line of credit or cash inside life insurance policies are commonly accessible choices.

Solution 2: Utilizing balance transfer cards to consolidate debt can decrease interest.

Scenario 2:

Car loan interest rate	3%
Mortgage interest rate	4%
Student loan interest rate	2.5%

Problem: Waiting to invest until all debt is paid

Solution: If it's possible to earn a high return in the market or other investment opportunities, don't rush to pay off low rate debt in advance. For example, if you generate 8% in the market and are paying 4% on the mortgage, the surplus is 4%. Simultaneously balancing debt payments and investing will allow you the opportunity to build wealth.

CHAPTER FOUR
Building Wealth: Construction Ahead

Constructing a prudent financial foundation leads to stability for the future. Appropriate building blocks need to be correctly placed, such as putting money to work early and often resulting in wealth accumulation. Your capital multiplies faster thanks to the magic of **compound interest**.

Compound Interest Comparison:

Name	Jordan
Current Age	<u>21</u>
Investing	$600/monthly
Period	39 years (Age 60)
Growth Rate	6%
Compounded	monthly
Jordan's End Balance	$1,124,098.63
Interest Earned	**$843,298.62**

Name	Aaron
Current Age	<u>30</u>
Investing	$600/monthly
Period	30 years (Age 60)
Growth Rate	6%
Compounded	monthly

Aaron's End Balance	$605,722.57
Interest Earned	**$389,722.57**

Now that you recognize the power of combining early investing and compound interest, ask yourself the following questions:

1.   What is my risk tolerance?

2.   Which investment account(s) should I consider?

Figure 2 illustrates the three risk management categories of investing:

15

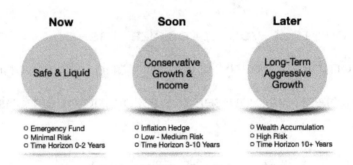

Figure 2

Risk Management Categories

Now

Safe & Liquid

o Emergency Fund
o Minimal Risk
o Time Horizon 0-2 Years

Soon

Conservative
Growth &
Income

o Inflation Hedge
o Low - Medium Risk
o Time Horizon 3-10 Years

Later

Long-Term
Aggressive
Growth

o Wealth Accumulation
o High Risk
o Time Horizon 10+ Years

Figure 3 lists various investment accounts. Tax features are the key differentiators.

Figure 3

Investment Accounts

Pre-Tax Dollars	Post-Tax Dollars	Tax-Advantaged Dollars
• 401(k) / 403(b) • SEP / SIMPLE IRA • Pensions • Traditional IRA • Qualified Annuity	• Brokerage Accounts • Bank Accounts • Real Estate • Alternatives • Non-Qualified Annuity	• Roth 401(k) / 403(b) • Roth IRA • 529 • Cash Value Life Insurance • Municipal Bond Interest
Features	**Features**	**Features**
• Tax-deferred growth • Distributions are taxed as income (penalties may apply)	• Capital gains are taxable • Dividends/Interest may be taxable	• Tax-free growth • Distributions are tax-free (rules may apply)

Choosing the right combination of accounts is a significant aspect of investment decision-making due to certain tax benefits.

Pre-tax dollars: Contributions are tax-deductible (not included in income), distributions are taxable at future income tax rates

Example:

Income	$100,000
Traditional 401(k) contribution	$10,000
Taxable income	**$90,000**

Tax-advantaged dollars: Contributions are not tax-deductible (included in income), distributions are tax-free (meeting specific requirements)

Example:

Income	$100,000
Roth 401(k) contribution	$10,000
Taxable income	**$100,000**

Roth 401(k)s, Roth 403(b)s, Roth IRAs, and cash value life insurance are excellent options for people who anticipate being in a higher tax bracket in the future.

Maximizing Future Tax Planning Example:

Traditional 401(k) (Pre-tax)

Name	Tyler
Current tax bracket	25%
Future tax bracket	30%
Initial investment	$20,000
Number of years	20
Account future value	$100,000 ($20,000 to $100,000 = 400% return)

Taxes paid on distribution of $100,000	$30,000 ($100,000 X .30)
Net balance	**$70,000**

Roth 401(k) (Tax-advantaged)

Name	Stevie
Current tax bracket	25%
Future tax bracket	30%
Initial investment	$15,000 ($20,000 less 25% paid in taxes)
Number of years	20
Account future value	$75,000 ($15,000 to $75,000 = 400% return)

Taxes paid on distribution of $75,000	<u>None</u>
Net balance	**$75,000**

The single largest expense in retirement can be taxes.

Taxable Retirement Assets may include:

1. Social Security

2. Pre-tax distributions

3. Annuity distributions

4. Marketable securities (Stocks, Bonds, ETFs, etc.)

5. Alternatives (Real estate, Hedge funds, Private equity)

Taxable gains and income received from these investments can potentially place you in a higher tax bracket. Utilizing tax-advantaged vehicles will remove the government from your retirement plan.

Consulting a tax advisor is recommended before finalizing a plan.

CHAPTER FIVE

Investments: The All-You-Can-Eat-Buffet

Investments are similar to an "all-you-can-eat buffet" because many options are available.

Figure 4

All-You-Can-Eat-Buffet
(Asset Classes)

Cash	US Equities	US Fixed-Income	Commodities	Alternatives	Global Markets
Checking / Savings	Large-Cap	Gov-Issued Securities	Gold	Real Estate	International Equities
T-Bills	Mid-Cap	Corporate-Issued Securities	Silver	Hedge Funds	International Fixed-Income
Commercial Paper	Small-Cap	Inflation-Protected Securities	Oil	Venture Capital	International Alternatives
Short-Term Gov Bonds	Micro-Cap	Mortgage-Backed Securities	Natural Gas	Private Equity	
Short-Term CDs	REITs	Asset-Backed Securities	Corn	Derivatives	
Money Market Funds	MLPs	Municipal Bonds	Soybeans	Collectibles	
Cash Value Life Insurance					

Diversification is a technique that mixes a wide variety of investments within a portfolio. The purpose is to reduce volatility by limiting exposure to any single asset or risk. Figure 5 demonstrates how individual asset classes go in and out of favor over time. When investors try to build their own portfolios, they sometimes dismiss asset classes that can be highly effective in providing diversification and smoothing returns.

Figure 5

Asset Class Returns

Ranked in order of performance from best to worst
(2009-2019)

	2009	2010	2011	2012	2013	2014	2015	2016	2017	2018	2019
BEST	Emerging Markets Equity 79.02%	Small Cap Growth 29.09%	REIT Index 9.37%	Emerging Markets Equity 18.63%	Small Cap Growth 43.30%	REIT Index 32.00%	Large Cap Growth 5.67%	Small Cap Value 31.74%	Emerging Markets Equity 37.75%	International Fixed Income 3.49%	Large Cap Growth 36.29%
	High Yield Bond 58.10%	REIT Index 28.07%	Emerging Market Debt 8.46%	Emerging Market Debt 18.54%	Small Cap Value 34.52%	Large Cap Value	REIT Index 4.48%	High Yield Bond 17.49%	Large Cap Growth 30.21%	Core Fixed Income 0.01%	Large Cap Core 31.43%
	Large Cap Growth 37.21%	Small Cap Value 24.50%	Core Fixed Income 7.84%	Small Cap Value 18.05%	Large Cap Growth 33.48%	Large Cap Core 13.24%	International Fixed Income 1.55%	Large Cap Value 17.34%	International Equity 25.62%	Large Cap Growth -1.51%	Small Cap Growth 28.48%
	Small Cap Growth 34.47%	Emerging Markets Equity 19.20%	High Yield Bond 4.37%	International Equity 17.90%	Large Cap Core 33.11%	Large Cap Growth 13.05%	Emerging Market Debt 1.23%	Large Cap Core 12.05%	Small Cap Growth 22.17%	High Yield Bond -2.27%	Large Cap Value 26.54%
	International Equity 32.46%	Large Cap Growth 16.71%	International Fixed Income 4.06%	Large Cap Value 17.51%	Large Cap Value 32.53%	International Fixed Income 9.77%	Large Cap Core 0.92%	Emerging Markets Equity 11.60%	Large Cap Core 21.69%	REIT Index -4.22%	REIT Index 23.00%
	REIT Index 28.00%	Large Cap Core 15.07%	Large Cap Growth 2.64%	REIT Index 13.60%	International Equity 23.29%	60/40 Diversified Portfolio 7.55%	Core Fixed Income 0.55%	Small Cap Growth 11.32%	60/40 Diversified Portfolio 15.68%	60/40 Diversified Portfolio -4.50%	Small Cap Value 22.39%
	Large Cap Core 28.43%	High Yield Bond 15.07%	Large Cap Core 1.50%	Large Cap Core 16.42%	60/40 Diversified Portfolio 16.52%	Core Fixed Income 5.97%	60/40 Diversified Portfolio -0.24%	60/40 Diversified Portfolio 10.19%	REIT Index 5.06%	Emerging Market Debt -4.61%	International Equity 22.01%
	Emerging Market Debt 28.18%	Large Cap Core 15.06%	60/40 Diversified Portfolio 0.70%	High Yield Bond 15.55%	High Yield Bond 7.41%	Small Cap Growth 5.60%	International Equity -0.39%	60/40 Diversified Portfolio 8.77%	Emerging Market Debt 9.32%	Large Cap Core -4.78%	60/40 Diversified Portfolio 20.97%
	60/40 Diversified Portfolio 26.28%	60/40 Diversified Portfolio 12.83%	International Equity 0.00%	Large Cap Growth 15.26%	International Fixed Income 1.42%	Emerging Market Debt 5.53%	Small Cap Growth -1.38%	Large Cap Growth 7.08%	Small Cap Value 7.84%	REIT Index -7.7%	Emerging Markets Equity 18.42%
	Small Cap Value 20.58%	Emerging Market Debt 12.04%	Small Cap Growth 2.91%	Small Cap Growth 14.59%	REIT Index 1.97%	Small Cap Value 4.22%	Large Cap Value -4.0%	High Yield Bond 6.16%	High Yield Bond 7.48%	Small Cap Growth -9.31%	Emerging Market Debt 14.42%
	Large Cap Value 19.60%	International Equity 8.21%	Small Cap Value 5.50%	60/40 Diversified Portfolio 13.41%	Core Fixed Income 2.02%	High Yield Bond 2.51%	High Yield Bond -4.61%	International Fixed Income 5.13%	REIT Index 5.00%	Small Cap Value -12.86%	High Yield Bond 14.41%
	Core Fixed Income 5.93%	Core Fixed Income 6.54%	International Equity -11.73%	International Fixed Income 6.9%	Emerging Markets Equity -2.27%	Emerging Markets Equity -1.82%	Small Cap Value -7.47%	Core Fixed Income 2.88%	Core Fixed Income 3.54%	International Equity -13.79%	Core Fixed Income 8.72%
WORST	International Fixed Income 2.38%	International Fixed Income 2.48%	Emerging Markets Equity -18.17%	Core Fixed Income 4.21%	Emerging Market Debt -6.58%	International Equity -4.48%	Emerging Markets Equity -14.6%	International Equity 1.51%	International Fixed Income 2.06%	Emerging Markets Equity -14.58%	International Fixed Income 8.02%

25

Source: Ibbotson Associates. This material has been obtained from sources generally considered reliable. No guarantee can be made as to its accuracy. Not intended to represent the performance of any particular investment.

As you can see, no single asset class remained at the top for two consecutive years. That is why it is important to work with a financial advisor to determine the proper asset allocation that suits your risk tolerance, lifestyle, and goals. Use the topics below to guide your advisor interview process.

Topics:

1. Experience

2. Investment philosophy and process

3. Educational background and credentials

4.   Services provided

5.   Communication frequency

6.   Performance track record

7.   Fees

CHAPTER SIX

Estate Planning: Preparing for the Inevitable

Estate planning generally gets overlooked. It is the process of transferring your assets to loved ones or charitable organizations after death. If implemented correctly, you can prevent family members from pulling out their hair. To get started, utilize the Estate Planning Checklist below.

Estate Planning Checklist:

1. Will – A legal declaration of a person's desires expressing how to distribute their estate after death. Passing away without a will results in Intestate Succession, which means the state creates one for you.

    a. Questions to consider:

        i. Whom do I choose to inherit my assets?

        ii. How do I divide my estate?

2. Probate – The legal procedure in which the court reviews the validity of the will. It also oversees

the administration and final distribution of assets.

a. Advantages of probate:

    i. Creditor protection

    ii. Fair estate appraisal

    iii. Distributes assets not stated in the will

b. Disadvantages of probate:

    i. Attorney fees

    ii. Court fees

    iii. Time-consuming

    iv. Public exposure

3. <u>Guardianship</u> – A person or entity designated in a will or appointed by a court to be responsible for minors or incapacitated adults.

    a. Questions to consider:

        i. Whom do I trust to safeguard my loved ones?

4. <u>Financial Power of Attorney</u> – A legal document granting a trusted person the authority to act on someone's behalf regarding financial matters while incapacitated.

a. Questions to consider:

    i. Whom do I trust that is most qualified to perform fiduciary responsibilities?

5. <u>Medical Power of Attorney</u> – A legal document granting a trusted person the ability to make healthcare decisions and communicate with medical personnel on someone's behalf while incapacitated.

a. Questions to consider:

    i. Which person is most capable of overseeing my medical care?

    ii.   Does the appointed person's thinking towards healthcare coincide with mine?

6. <u>Beneficiary</u> – A person(s) or entity receiving a designated asset upon someone's death. By naming a beneficiary, probate will be avoided.

    a.   Questions to consider:

        i.   Whom should I designate as a beneficiary?

        ii.   What percentage of assets will the beneficiary inherit?

7. <u>Living (Revocable) Trust</u> – A legal document designating a trustee to manage an individual's assets during their lifetime to benefit a beneficiary.

    a. Advantages of a living trust:

        i.   Avoids probate

        ii. Protects privacy

        iii. Option to amend planning

        iv. Creditor protection

    b. Disadvantages of a living trust:

        i.   Attorney fees

        ii. Lack of tax advantages

        iii. More complex to draft

c. Questions to consider:

    i. How can a living trust add value to my estate plan?

    ii. Who is best suited to be the trustee?

8. <u>Life Insurance Integration</u> – Utilizing life insurance to leave income tax-free money to beneficiaries and reduce estate taxes.

a. Questions to consider:

    i. Do I need life insurance?

    ii. How much insurance is necessary?

9. <u>Business Succession Planning</u> – The process of transferring business interests to ensure the continuation of a company.

    a. Questions to consider:

        i. Who is best suited to succeed me?

        ii. What is the most efficient method to transfer my business interest?

10. <u>Federal/State Estate Tax</u> – A tax imposed on an estate whose value exceeds the federal/state government's lifetime exemption. Only the amount above the exemption is subject to tax.

a.   Questions to consider:

i.   After death, what will be my federal/state tax liability?

ii. When is the estate tax due?

11. <u>Advanced Planning Techniques</u> – Complex strategies to reduce an estate's net worth, limit taxes, and leave a legacy.

a. Irrevocable trusts

b. Gifting strategies

c. Generation-skipping

d. Charitable giving

Consult with a financial advisor and estate planning attorney to collaborate, create, and execute your plan.

CHAPTER SEVEN

Life Insurance: The Greatest Gift

Accepting one's mortality is a part of life. Being proactive and insuring yourself is the greatest gift of love. Providing your family the ability to sustain the same quality of life after your death will give you peace of mind. In addition, life insurance can solve business continuation concerns. Premiums are paid to guarantee an income-tax-free death benefit for beneficiaries.

Benefits of Life Insurance:

1. Salary/Income replacement

2. Income tax-free death benefit

3. Debt elimination

4. Pays for funeral and burial costs

5. Pays for estate taxes

6. Pays for medical expenses

7. Pays for childcare expenses

8. Pays for education expenses

9. Tax-deferred growth

10. Tax-free withdrawals up to basis

11. Tax-free loans

12. Business overhead/buyout

13. Key employee protection

The two types of life insurance are **term** and **permanent**.

Term Insurance: Guarantees a death benefit for a stated period of time

Advantages:

1. Affordable

   a. Less expensive premiums

2. Death benefit

   a. Income tax-free

3. Simplicity

   a. Easy to understand and compare rates

4. Temporary coverage

    a. Specific expenses can be paid such as a funeral, childcare, and education expenses

5. Convertibility clause

    a. The insured can exchange an existing policy for a permanent one regardless of health

Disadvantages:

1. No cash value

    a. Doesn't include a savings/ investment feature

2. At expiration, coverage ends

    a. Health issues can make it difficult to purchase a new policy

    b. New policy premiums will be more expensive

3. Claims

    a. Approximately 2% of term policies end in a death claim

Permanent Insurance: Provides **lifelong** death benefit protection and includes a savings/investment component

Advantages:

1. Fixed premiums

   a. The payment amount remains the same over the lifetime of the policy

2. Death benefit

   a. Income tax-free

3. Policy options

   a. Whole Life

   b. Universal Life

   c. Variable Life

   d. Indexed Universal Life

4. Cash value

    a. A portion of each premium payment is allocated into a separate savings/ investment account

    b. Tax-free accumulation

    c. Tax-free withdrawals up to basis

    d. Tax-free loans

    e. Can be leveraged as collateral

Disadvantages:

1. Higher premiums

    a. Lifelong coverage and a cash value feature cause a more expensive policy

2.   Loans

    a.   An outstanding balance will reduce the death benefit

    b.   A high-interest rate could be charged until the loan is repaid

3.   Potential losses

    a.   Policies that have separate investment accounts might lose money due to poor market performance

The case below demonstrates a calculation to determine the death benefit needed for income replacement and debt elimination.

Name	Dan
Marital status	Married
Gross income	$100,000
Kids	2
Debt	Mortgage $400,000, miscellaneous liabilities $50,000
College tuition	$200,000
Medical bills	$20,000
Funeral cost	$15,000
Rate of return	5%

Step 1: Using a 5% rate of return, calculate the amount of money that will generate $100,000 of income

    b. $100,000 / .05 = $2 million death benefit

Step 2: Add debt and expenses

    c. $2 million + $400,000 mortgage + $50,000 miscellaneous liabilities + $200,000 tuition + $20,000 medical bills + $15,000 funeral costs = **$2,485,000 total death benefit**

Figure 6

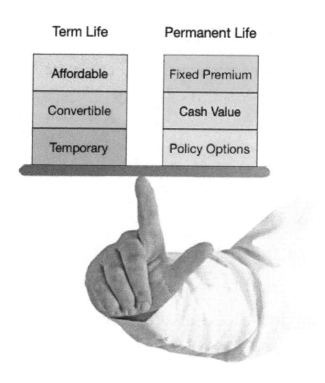

Most people are underinsured and
don't realize it!

CHAPTER EIGHT

Disability Insurance: Protecting the Most Valuable Asset...YOU

There is one asset that is always excluded from the balance sheet...YOU! Your ability to generate income is commonly taken for granted. Picture being hurt or sick and unable to work. How would you earn your next paycheck? Which account would you withdraw from to pay the bills? (e.g., emergency savings, college fund, retirement accounts)

The solution is Disability Insurance! In the event of becoming incapable of working, it provides approximately 60% of a salary. The two types of policies are **short** and **long term**. Short term offers coverage for three to six months. Long term extends payments six months or more.

Employer-paid premiums result in taxable benefits to employees. Conversely, employee-paid premiums result in tax-free benefits. If coverage isn't offered at work, individual private policies are available.

Disability Monthly Benefit Example:

Kendra	Disabled
Salary	$60,000
Annual Benefit (60%)	$36,000 ($60,000 X .60)
Monthly Benefit	**$3,000** ($36,000 / 12)

Kendra just received her disability benefit. Doesn't she look relieved!

CONCLUSION

Achieving financial stability allows you the freedom to pursue passions and spend time with loved ones. It is essential to design, implement, and monitor a strategic plan. If done well, you will **WIN** the financial planning game!

ABOUT THE AUTHOR

Ethan Schmidt assists individuals in designing a winning financial game plan to achieve personal goals. He is a CERTIFIED FINANCIAL PLANNER™ and a Chartered Retirement Planning Counselor®. Beginning his career at Merrill, A Bank of America Company, he provided personalized unbiased advice to individuals and families to improve their financial situation. Ethan was recognized as a top advisor.

He then joined his father's boutique insurance and estate planning business in Chicago to further pursue his entrepreneurial ambitions.

He subsequently created an investment division called Catalyst Wealth Management. As President and Partner, he takes pride in building long-lasting relationships and has a unique ability to design customized portfolios. Ethan focuses on concepts that will guide and reveal how to WIN the financial planning game.

FOLLOW ME AT

/financialadvisorcfp

/ethancfp

Email – ethan@schmidtfinancial.com

Catalyst Wealth Management Website -

https://catalystwealthmgmt.com/

CPSIA information can be obtained
at www.ICGtesting.com
Printed in the USA
LVHW080926241120
672561LV00010B/504